Fishing Log

Location:________________________ Date:

Location Details: ________________

____

Companions:____________________

Water Temp:_________ Air Temp:______

Hours Fished:_______ Wind Direction:_______

WInd Speed:_______ Humidity:_______

Weather ☼ ⚡ ________________________________

Moon Phase:________________________________

Tide Phase:________________________________

Notes:________________________________

Species:	Bait:	Length:	Weight:	Time:

Other Notes:

Other Notes:

Other Notes:

Other Notes:

Fishing Log

Location:_______________________ Date:______________

Location Details: ___________________________________

____

Companions:____

Water Temp:__________ Air Temp:________

Hours Fished:________ Wind Direction:________

WInd Speed:________ Humidity:________

Weather ☀ ⚡ _______________________________________

Moon Phase:____

Tide Phase:____

Notes:____

Species:	Bait:	Length:	Weight:	Time:

Other Notes:

Other Notes:

Other Notes:

Other Notes:

Fishing Log

Location:________________________ Date:______________

Location Details: ________________________________

____

Companions:______________________________________

Water Temp:___________ Air Temp:_________

Hours Fished:_________ Wind Direction:________

WInd Speed:_________ Humidity:________

Weather ☀ ⚡ ________________________________

Moon Phase:______________________________________

Tide Phase:______________________________________

Notes:____

Species:	Bait:	Length:	Weight:	Time:

Other Notes:

Other Notes:

Other Notes:

Other Notes:

Fishing Log

Location:________________________ Date:______________

Location Details: ___________________________________

____

Companions:____

Water Temp:__________ Air Temp:_________

Hours Fished:_________ Wind Direction:_______

WInd Speed:________ Humidity:_______

Weather ☀ ⚡ ____

Moon Phase:____

Tide Phase:____

Notes:____

Species:	Bait:	Length:	Weight:	Time:

Other Notes:

Other Notes:

Other Notes:

Other Notes:

Fishing Log

Location:_________________________ Date:______________
Location Details: ____
____
Companions:____
Water Temp:__________ Air Temp:_________
Hours Fished:________ Wind Direction:________
WInd Speed:________ Humidity:________

Weather ☀ ⚡ ____
Moon Phase:____
Tide Phase:____
Notes:____

Species:	Bait:	Length:	Weight:	Time:

Other Notes:

Other Notes:

Other Notes:

Other Notes:

Fishing Log

Location:_______________________ Date:_______________

Location Details: ___________________________________

____

Companions:_______________________________________

Water Temp:___________ Air Temp:_________

Hours Fished:_________ Wind Direction:_________

WInd Speed:_________ Humidity:_________

Weather ☼ ⚡ _______________________________________

Moon Phase:____

Tide Phase:____

Notes:____

Species:	Bait:	Length:	Weight:	Time:
Other Notes:				
Other Notes:				
Other Notes:				
Other Notes:				

Fishing Log

Location:_________________________ Date:_______________

Location Details: _______________________________________

____

Companions:____

Water Temp:___________ Air Temp:_________

Hours Fished:________ Wind Direction:________

WInd Speed:________ Humidity:________

Weather ☼ ⚡ _______________________________________

Moon Phase:____

Tide Phase:____

Notes:____

Species:	Bait:	Length:	Weight:	Time:

Other Notes:

Other Notes:

Other Notes:

Other Notes:

Fishing Log

Location:________________________ Date:_____________

Location Details: ________________________

____

Companions:________________________________

Water Temp:__________ Air Temp:________

Hours Fished:________ Wind Direction:________

WInd Speed:________ Humidity:________

Weather ☀ ⚡ ________________________________

Moon Phase:________________________________

Tide Phase:________________________________

Notes:________________________________

Species:	Bait:	Length:	Weight:	Time:

Other Notes:

Other Notes:

Other Notes:

Other Notes:

Fishing Log

Location:_________________________ Date:_______________

Location Details: ______________________________________

____

Companions:____

Water Temp:__________ Air Temp:________

Hours Fished:________ Wind Direction:________

WInd Speed:________ Humidity:_______

Weather ☀ ⚡ _______________________________________

Moon Phase:____

Tide Phase:____

Notes:____

Species:	Bait:	Length:	Weight:	Time:
Other Notes:				
Other Notes:				
Other Notes:				
Other Notes:				

Fishing Log

Location:_________________________ Date:______________
Location Details: ______________________________________

____
Companions:____
Water Temp:__________ Air Temp:________
Hours Fished:________ Wind Direction:_______
WInd Speed:________ Humidity:_______

Weather ☼ ⚡ ____
Moon Phase:____
Tide Phase:____
Notes:____

Species:	Bait:	Length:	Weight:	Time:
Other Notes:				
Other Notes:				
Other Notes:				
Other Notes:				

Fishing Log

Location:_________________________ Date:_______________

Location Details: ____

____

Companions:____

Water Temp:__________ Air Temp:_________

Hours Fished:_________ Wind Direction:_______

WInd Speed:_________ Humidity:_______

Weather ☀ ⚡ _______________________________________

Moon Phase:____

Tide Phase:____

Notes:____

Species:	Bait:	Length:	Weight:	Time:

Other Notes:

Other Notes:

Other Notes:

Other Notes:

Fishing Log

Location:_______________________ Date:_______________

Location Details: _________________________________

____

Companions:_____________________________________

Water Temp:__________ Air Temp:_________

Hours Fished:________ Wind Direction:________

WInd Speed:________ Humidity:________

Weather ____

Moon Phase:_____________________________________

Tide Phase:______________________________________

Notes:____

Species:	Bait:	Length:	Weight:	Time:

Other Notes:

Other Notes:

Other Notes:

Other Notes:

Fishing Log

Location:_________________________ Date:_______________

Location Details: ____

____

Companions:____

Water Temp:__________ Air Temp:_________

Hours Fished:________ Wind Direction:________

WInd Speed:________ Humidity:________

Weather ☀ ⚡ ____

Moon Phase:____

Tide Phase:____

Notes:____

Species:	Bait:	Length:	Weight:	Time:

Other Notes:

Other Notes:

Other Notes:

Other Notes:

Fishing Log

Location:_________________________ Date:_______________

Location Details: ______________________________________

____

Companions:____

Water Temp:___________ Air Temp:_________

Hours Fished:_________ Wind Direction:_________

WInd Speed:_________ Humidity:_________

Weather ☀️⚡ ____

Moon Phase:____

Tide Phase:____

Notes:____

Species:	Bait:	Length:	Weight:	Time:

Other Notes:

| | | | | |

Other Notes:

| | | | | |

Other Notes:

| | | | | |

Other Notes:

| | | | | |

Fishing Log

Location:_____________________ Date:_____________

Location Details: _________________________________

____

Companions:______________________________________

Water Temp:__________ Air Temp:_________

Hours Fished:________ Wind Direction:________

WInd Speed:________ Humidity:_______

Weather ☼ ⚡ ____

Moon Phase:______________________________________

Tide Phase:_______________________________________

Notes:____

Species:	Bait:	Length:	Weight:	Time:

Other Notes:

Other Notes:

Other Notes:

Other Notes:

Fishing Log

Location:______________________ Date:______________

Location Details: ___________________________________

____

Companions:____

Water Temp:__________ Air Temp:________

Hours Fished:________ Wind Direction:________

WInd Speed:________ Humidity:________

Weather ☼ ⚡ ____

Moon Phase:____

Tide Phase:____

Notes:____

Species:	Bait:	Length:	Weight:	Time:
Other Notes:				
Other Notes:				
Other Notes:				
Other Notes:				

Fishing Log

Location:_________________________ Date:______________
Location Details: ____

____
Companions:____
Water Temp:__________ Air Temp:________
Hours Fished:________ Wind Direction:________
WInd Speed:________ Humidity:________

Weather ☼ ⚡ ____
Moon Phase:____
Tide Phase:____
Notes:____

Species:	Bait:	Length:	Weight:	Time:

Other Notes:

Other Notes:

Other Notes:

Other Notes:

Fishing Log

Location:________________________ Date:______________

Location Details: ______________________________________

____

Companions:____

Water Temp:__________ Air Temp:________

Hours Fished:________ Wind Direction:________

WInd Speed:________ Humidity:________

Weather ☼ ⚡ ______________________________________

Moon Phase:____

Tide Phase:____

Notes:____

Species:	Bait:	Length:	Weight:	Time:

Other Notes:

Other Notes:

Other Notes:

Other Notes:

Fishing Log

Location:________________________ Date:_______________

Location Details: ______________________________________

____

Companions:____

Water Temp:__________ Air Temp:__________

Hours Fished:________ Wind Direction:________

WInd Speed:________ Humidity:________

Weather ☀⚡ ____

Moon Phase:____

Tide Phase:____

Notes:____

Species:	Bait:	Length:	Weight:	Time:

Other Notes:

Other Notes:

Other Notes:

Other Notes:

Fishing Log

Location:_________________________ Date:_______________

Location Details: _____________________________________

____

Companions:____

Water Temp:__________ Air Temp:________

Hours Fished:________ Wind Direction:________

WInd Speed:________ Humidity:________

Weather ☀⚡ ____

Moon Phase:____

Tide Phase:____

Notes:____

Species:	Bait:	Length:	Weight:	Time:

Other Notes:

Other Notes:

Other Notes:

Other Notes:

Fishing Log

Location:________________________ Date:______________

Location Details: ___________________________________

____

Companions:____

Water Temp:__________ Air Temp:_________

Hours Fished:________ Wind Direction:________

WInd Speed:________ Humidity:________

Weather ☀ ⚡ ____

Moon Phase:____

Tide Phase:____

Notes:____

Species:	Bait:	Length:	Weight:	Time:

Other Notes:

Other Notes:

Other Notes:

Other Notes:

Fishing Log

Location:_____________________ Date:_____________

Location Details: _________________________________

____

Companions:______________________________________

Water Temp:__________ Air Temp:________

Hours Fished:________ Wind Direction:________

WInd Speed:________ Humidity:________

Weather ____

Moon Phase:______________________________________

Tide Phase:_______________________________________

Notes:____

Species:	Bait:	Length:	Weight:	Time:
Other Notes:				
Other Notes:				
Other Notes:				
Other Notes:				

Fishing Log

Location:________________________ Date:____________

Location Details: ________________________________

____

Companions:______________________________________

Water Temp:__________ Air Temp:________

Hours Fished:________ Wind Direction:________

WInd Speed:________ Humidity:________

Weather ☀⚡ _______________________________

Moon Phase:______________________________________

Tide Phase:______________________________________

Notes:____

Species:	Bait:	Length:	Weight:	Time:

Other Notes:

Other Notes:

Other Notes:

Other Notes:

Fishing Log

Location:________________________ Date:______________

Location Details: _______________________________

____

Companions:_____________________________________

Water Temp:__________ Air Temp:________

Hours Fished:________ Wind Direction:________

WInd Speed:________ Humidity:________

Weather ☼ ⚡ _______________________________

Moon Phase:_____________________________________

Tide Phase:_____________________________________

Notes:____

Species:	Bait:	Length:	Weight:	Time:
Other Notes:				
Other Notes:				
Other Notes:				
Other Notes:				

Fishing Log

Location:_________________________ Date:_______________

Location Details: ____

____

Companions:____

Water Temp:__________ Air Temp:_________

Hours Fished:_________ Wind Direction:________

WInd Speed:_________ Humidity:________

Weather ☀ ⚡ ____

Moon Phase:____

Tide Phase:____

Notes:____

Species:	Bait:	Length:	Weight:	Time:

Other Notes:

Other Notes:

Other Notes:

Other Notes:

Fishing Log

Location:_________________________ Date:_______________

Location Details: _________________________________

____

Companions:_______________________________________

Water Temp:__________ Air Temp:________

Hours Fished:________ Wind Direction:________

WInd Speed:________ Humidity:________

Weather ☼ ⚡ _________________________________

Moon Phase:____

Tide Phase:____

Notes:____

Species:	Bait:	Length:	Weight:	Time:

Other Notes:

Other Notes:

Other Notes:

Other Notes:

Fishing Log

Location:_________________________ Date:_______________

Location Details: _________________________________

____

Companions:______________________________________

Water Temp:__________ Air Temp:________

Hours Fished:________ Wind Direction:________

WInd Speed:________ Humidity:________

Weather ☼ ⚡ ____

Moon Phase:______________________________________

Tide Phase:_______________________________________

Notes:____

Species:	Bait:	Length:	Weight:	Time:
Other Notes:				
Other Notes:				
Other Notes:				
Other Notes:				

Fishing Log

Location:_______________________ Date:_____________

Location Details: _________________________________

____

Companions:______________________________________

Water Temp:__________ Air Temp:_________

Hours Fished:________ Wind Direction:________

WInd Speed:________ Humidity:________

Weather ☀ ⚡ _________________________________

Moon Phase:______________________________________

Tide Phase:_______________________________________

Notes:____

Species:	Bait:	Length:	Weight:	Time:

Other Notes:

Other Notes:

Other Notes:

Other Notes:

Fishing Log

Location:_________________________ Date:______________
Location Details: ____________________________________

____

Companions:____
Water Temp:__________ Air Temp:________
Hours Fished:_______ Wind Direction:_______
WInd Speed:_______ Humidity:_______

Weather ☼ ⚡ ____
Moon Phase:____
Tide Phase:____
Notes:____

Species:	Bait:	Length:	Weight:	Time:

Other Notes:

Other Notes:

Other Notes:

Other Notes:

Fishing Log

Location:_____________________________ Date:_______________

Location Details: ____

____

Companions:____

Water Temp:__________ Air Temp:________

Hours Fished:________ Wind Direction:________

WInd Speed:________ Humidity:________

Weather ☼ ⚡ ____

Moon Phase:____

Tide Phase:____

Notes:____

Species:	Bait:	Length:	Weight:	Time:

Other Notes:

Other Notes:

Other Notes:

Other Notes:

Fishing Log

Location:_________________________ Date:_______________
Location Details: _______________________________________

____
Companions:____
Water Temp:___________ Air Temp:_________
Hours Fished:_________ Wind Direction:________
WInd Speed:_________ Humidity:________

Weather ☼ ⚡ ____
Moon Phase:____
Tide Phase:____
Notes:____

Species:	Bait:	Length:	Weight:	Time:

Other Notes:

Other Notes:

Other Notes:

Other Notes:

Fishing Log

Location:________________________ Date:______________

Location Details: ______________________________

____

Companions:_____________________________________

Water Temp:__________ Air Temp:________

Hours Fished:________ Wind Direction:________

WInd Speed:________ Humidity:________

Weather ☀⚡ _______________________________

Moon Phase:_____________________________________

Tide Phase:_____________________________________

Notes:____

Species:	Bait:	Length:	Weight:	Time:

Other Notes:

Other Notes:

Other Notes:

Other Notes:

Fishing Log

Location:_________________________ Date:______________

Location Details: ____

____

Companions:____

Water Temp:__________ Air Temp:________

Hours Fished:________ Wind Direction:________

WInd Speed:________ Humidity:________

Weather ☼ ⚡ _______________________________________

Moon Phase:____

Tide Phase:____

Notes:____

Species:	Bait:	Length:	Weight:	Time:

Other Notes:

Other Notes:

Other Notes:

Other Notes:

Fishing Log

Location:_________________________ Date:_____________
Location Details: ___________________________________

____
Companions:____
Water Temp:___________ Air Temp:_________
Hours Fished:__________ Wind Direction:_________
WInd Speed:_________ Humidity:________

Weather ☀ ⚡ ____
Moon Phase:____
Tide Phase:____
Notes:____

Species:	Bait:	Length:	Weight:	Time:
Other Notes:				
Other Notes:				
Other Notes:				
Other Notes:				

Fishing Log

Location:________________________ Date:______________

Location Details: _____________________________________

____

Companions:____

Water Temp:__________ Air Temp:_________

Hours Fished:________ Wind Direction:________

WInd Speed:________ Humidity:________

Weather ☀ ⚡ ____

Moon Phase:____

Tide Phase:____

Notes:____

Species:	Bait:	Length:	Weight:	Time:

Other Notes:

Other Notes:

Other Notes:

Other Notes:

Fishing Log

Location:________________________ Date:______________

Location Details: _________________________________

____

Companions:______________________________________

Water Temp:__________ Air Temp:_________

Hours Fished:_________ Wind Direction:_________

WInd Speed:_________ Humidity:_________

Weather ☀ ⚡ _________________________________

Moon Phase:______________________________________

Tide Phase:_______________________________________

Notes:____

Species:	Bait:	Length:	Weight:	Time:
Other Notes:				
Other Notes:				
Other Notes:				
Other Notes:				

Fishing Log

Location:_________________________ Date:_______________

Location Details: _______________________________________

____

Companions:____

Water Temp:__________ Air Temp:_________

Hours Fished:________ Wind Direction:________

WInd Speed:________ Humidity:________

Weather ☀ ⚡ ____

Moon Phase:____

Tide Phase:____

Notes:____

Species:	Bait:	Length:	Weight:	Time:
Other Notes:				
Other Notes:				
Other Notes:				
Other Notes:				

Fishing Log

Location:_________________________ Date:_______________
Location Details: ____________________________________
____
Companions:____
Water Temp:___________ Air Temp:_________
Hours Fished:________ Wind Direction:________
WInd Speed:________ Humidity:________

Weather ☼ ⚡ ______________________________________
Moon Phase:____
Tide Phase:____
Notes:____

Species:	Bait:	Length:	Weight:	Time:
Other Notes:				
Other Notes:				
Other Notes:				
Other Notes:				

Fishing Log

Location:_________________________ Date:_______________

Location Details: _________________________________

____

Companions:_______________________________________

Water Temp:__________ Air Temp:_________

Hours Fished:________ Wind Direction:________

WInd Speed:________ Humidity:________

Weather ☼ ⚡ _________________________________

Moon Phase:_______________________________________

Tide Phase:____

Notes:____

Species:	Bait:	Length:	Weight:	Time:
Other Notes:				
Other Notes:				
Other Notes:				
Other Notes:				

Fishing Log

Location:________________________ Date:____________

Location Details: ______________________________

____

Companions:____________________________________

Water Temp:__________ Air Temp:________

Hours Fished:________ Wind Direction:________

WInd Speed:________ Humidity:________

Weather ☼ ⚡ ______________________________

Moon Phase:____________________________________

Tide Phase:____________________________________

Notes:____

Species:	Bait:	Length:	Weight:	Time:

Other Notes:

Other Notes:

Other Notes:

Other Notes:

Fishing Log

Location:_____________________ Date:_____________

Location Details: _________________________________

____

Companions:_____________________________________

Water Temp:__________ Air Temp:________

Hours Fished:________ Wind Direction:________

WInd Speed:________ Humidity:________

Weather ☀ ⚡ ________________________________

Moon Phase:_____________________________________

Tide Phase:______________________________________

Notes:____

Species:	Bait:	Length:	Weight:	Time:

Other Notes:

Other Notes:

Other Notes:

Other Notes:

Fishing Log

Location:________________________ Date:____________

Location Details: _________________________________

____

Companions:______________________________________

Water Temp:__________ Air Temp:________

Hours Fished:________ Wind Direction:________

WInd Speed:________ Humidity:________

Weather ☀ ⚡ ___________________________________

Moon Phase:______________________________________

Tide Phase:_______________________________________

Notes:____

Species:	Bait:	Length:	Weight:	Time:

Other Notes:

| | | | | |

Other Notes:

| | | | | |

Other Notes:

| | | | | |

Other Notes:

| | | | | |

Fishing Log

Location:_________________________ Date:_______________
Location Details: _________________________________

____
Companions:_______________________________________
Water Temp:__________ Air Temp:_________
Hours Fished:_________ Wind Direction:_________
WInd Speed:_________ Humidity:_________

Weather ☀ ⚡ _______________________________________
Moon Phase:_______________________________________
Tide Phase:_______________________________________
Notes:____

Species:	Bait:	Length:	Weight:	Time:

Other Notes:

Other Notes:

Other Notes:

Other Notes:

Fishing Log

Location:_________________________ Date:_______________

Location Details: _______________________________________

____

Companions:____

Water Temp:___________ Air Temp:_________

Hours Fished:_________ Wind Direction:_________

WInd Speed:_________ Humidity:_________

Weather ☼ ⚡ ____

Moon Phase:____

Tide Phase:____

Notes:____

Species:	Bait:	Length:	Weight:	Time:

Other Notes:

Other Notes:

Other Notes:

Other Notes:

Fishing Log

Location:_______________________ Date:______________

Location Details: ___________________________________

____

Companions:____

Water Temp:__________ Air Temp:________

Hours Fished:________ Wind Direction:_______

WInd Speed:________ Humidity:_______

Weather ☀⚡ _______________________________________

Moon Phase:____

Tide Phase:____

Notes:____

Species:	Bait:	Length:	Weight:	Time:

Other Notes:

Other Notes:

Other Notes:

Other Notes:

Fishing Log

Location:_______________________ Date:_______________

Location Details: ___________________________________

____

Companions:____

Water Temp:__________ Air Temp:________

Hours Fished:________ Wind Direction:________

WInd Speed:________ Humidity:________

Weather ☼ ⚡ ____

Moon Phase:____

Tide Phase:____

Notes:____

Species:	Bait:	Length:	Weight:	Time:

Other Notes:

Other Notes:

Other Notes:

Other Notes:

Fishing Log

Location:___________________________ Date:_______________

Location Details: ____

____

Companions:____

Water Temp:___________ Air Temp:_________

Hours Fished:_________ Wind Direction:_________

WInd Speed:_________ Humidity:_________

Weather ☼ ⚡ ____

Moon Phase:____

Tide Phase: ____

Notes:____

Species:	Bait:	Length:	Weight:	Time:
Other Notes:				
Other Notes:				
Other Notes:				
Other Notes:				

Fishing Log

Location:_______________________ Date:_______________
Location Details: _________________________________

____
Companions:_______________________________________
Water Temp:___________ Air Temp:_________
Hours Fished:_________ Wind Direction:_________
WInd Speed:_________ Humidity:_________

Weather ☼ ⚡ _________________________________
Moon Phase:______________________________________
Tide Phase:_______________________________________
Notes:____

Species:	Bait:	Length:	Weight:	Time:

Other Notes:

Other Notes:

Other Notes:

Other Notes:

Fishing Log

Location:_____________________ Date:_____________

Location Details: _________________________________

____

Companions:_____________________________________

Water Temp:__________ Air Temp:________

Hours Fished:________ Wind Direction:________

WInd Speed:________ Humidity:________

Weather ☀⚡ ___________________________________

Moon Phase:_____________________________________

Tide Phase:_____________________________________

Notes:____

Species:	Bait:	Length:	Weight:	Time:

Other Notes:

Other Notes:

Other Notes:

Other Notes:

Fishing Log

Location:_________________________ Date:_______________

Location Details: ____

____

Companions:____

Water Temp:___________ Air Temp:_________

Hours Fished:_________ Wind Direction:_________

WInd Speed:_________ Humidity:_________

Weather ☼ ⚡ ____

Moon Phase:____

Tide Phase:____

Notes:____

Species:	Bait:	Length:	Weight:	Time:

Other Notes:

Other Notes:

Other Notes:

Other Notes:

Fishing Log

Location:_________________________ Date:_______________

Location Details: ____

____

Companions:____

Water Temp:___________ Air Temp:________

Hours Fished:_________ Wind Direction:_________

WInd Speed:_________ Humidity:________

Weather ☼ ⚡ ____

Moon Phase:____

Tide Phase:____

Notes:____

Species:	Bait:	Length:	Weight:	Time:

Other Notes:

Other Notes:

Other Notes:

Other Notes:

Fishing Log

Location:________________________ **Date:**______________

Location Details: ___________________________________

____

Companions:____

Water Temp:__________ **Air Temp:**________

Hours Fished:________ **Wind Direction:**________

WInd Speed:________ **Humidity:**________

Weather ☼ ⚡ ___________________________________

Moon Phase:____

Tide Phase:____

Notes:____

Species:	Bait:	Length:	Weight:	Time:

Other Notes:

Other Notes:

Other Notes:

Other Notes:

Fishing Log

Location:_____________________ Date:_____________

Location Details: _________________________________

____

Companions:_____________________________________

Water Temp:__________ Air Temp:________

Hours Fished:________ Wind Direction:________

WInd Speed:________ Humidity:________

Weather ☼ ⚡ _______________________________

Moon Phase:_____________________________________

Tide Phase:_____________________________________

Notes:____

Species:	Bait:	Length:	Weight:	Time:
Other Notes:				
Other Notes:				
Other Notes:				
Other Notes:				

Fishing Log

Location:___________________________ Date:_______________
Location Details: ___________________________________

____
Companions:____
Water Temp:___________ Air Temp:_________
Hours Fished:_________ Wind Direction:_________
WInd Speed:_________ Humidity:_________

Weather ☀ ⚡ _______________________________________
Moon Phase:____
Tide Phase:____
Notes:____

Species:	Bait:	Length:	Weight:	Time:

Other Notes:

Other Notes:

Other Notes:

Other Notes:

Fishing Log

Location:_____________________ Date:_____________

Location Details: ___________________________

____

Companions:________________________________

Water Temp:_________ Air Temp:________

Hours Fished:________ Wind Direction:_______

WInd Speed:________ Humidity:_______

Weather ☀⚡___________________________________

Moon Phase:_______________________________

Tide Phase:________________________________

Notes:____________________________________

Species:	Bait:	Length:	Weight:	Time:

Other Notes:

Other Notes:

Other Notes:

Other Notes:

Fishing Log

Location:_____________________ Date:_____________

Location Details: _________________________________

____

Companions:_______________________________________

Water Temp:__________ Air Temp:________

Hours Fished:________ Wind Direction:________

WInd Speed:________ Humidity:________

Weather ☼ ⚡ ________________________________

Moon Phase:_______________________________________

Tide Phase:____

Notes:____

Species:	Bait:	Length:	Weight:	Time:

Other Notes:

Other Notes:

Other Notes:

Other Notes:

Fishing Log

Location:__________________________ Date:_______________

Location Details: ___________________________________

____

Companions:____

Water Temp:___________ Air Temp:_________

Hours Fished:_________ Wind Direction:_________

WInd Speed:_________ Humidity:_________

Weather ☀ ⚡ ____

Moon Phase:____

Tide Phase:____

Notes:____

Species:	Bait:	Length:	Weight:	Time:

Other Notes:

Other Notes:

Other Notes:

Other Notes:

Fishing Log

Location:_____________________ Date:_____________

Location Details: _______________________________

____

Companions:_____________________________________

Water Temp:__________ Air Temp:________

Hours Fished:________ Wind Direction:________

WInd Speed:________ Humidity:________

Weather ☀ ⚡ _____________________________

Moon Phase:_____________________________________

Tide Phase:_____________________________________

Notes:____

Species:	Bait:	Length:	Weight:	Time:

Other Notes:

Other Notes:

Other Notes:

Other Notes:

Fishing Log

Location:_________________________ Date:_______________

Location Details: ____

____

Companions:____

Water Temp:___________ Air Temp:_________

Hours Fished:_________ Wind Direction:_________

WInd Speed:_________ Humidity:_________

Weather ☼ ⚡ ____

Moon Phase:____

Tide Phase:____

Notes:____

Species:	Bait:	Length:	Weight:	Time:

Other Notes:

Other Notes:

Other Notes:

Other Notes:

Fishing Log

Location:_____________________ Date:____________
Location Details: _________________________________
____
Companions:______________________________________
Water Temp:__________ Air Temp:________
Hours Fished:________ Wind Direction:________
WInd Speed:________ Humidity:________

Weather ☀ ⚡ _____________________________________
Moon Phase:______________________________________
Tide Phase:_______________________________________
Notes:____

Species:	Bait:	Length:	Weight:	Time:

Other Notes:

Other Notes:

Other Notes:

Other Notes:

Fishing Log

Location:_________________________ Date:______________
Location Details: ________________________________

____
Companions:____
Water Temp:__________ Air Temp:_________
Hours Fished:_________ Wind Direction:________
WInd Speed:_________ Humidity:________

Weather ☼ ⚡ ______________________________________
Moon Phase:____
Tide Phase:____
Notes:____

Species:	Bait:	Length:	Weight:	Time:

Other Notes:

Other Notes:

Other Notes:

Other Notes:

Fishing Log

Location:_________________________ Date:_______________

Location Details: ____

____

Companions:____

Water Temp:__________ Air Temp:________

Hours Fished:________ Wind Direction:________

WInd Speed:________ Humidity:________

Weather ☀⚡____

Moon Phase:____

Tide Phase:____

Notes:____

Species:	Bait:	Length:	Weight:	Time:

Other Notes:

Other Notes:

Other Notes:

Other Notes:

Fishing Log

Location:_________________________ Date:_______________

Location Details: _______________________________________

____

Companions:____

Water Temp:___________ Air Temp:__________

Hours Fished:__________ Wind Direction:__________

WInd Speed:__________ Humidity:__________

Weather ☼ ⚡ ____

Moon Phase:____

Tide Phase:____

Notes:____

Species:	Bait:	Length:	Weight:	Time:
Other Notes:				
Other Notes:				
Other Notes:				
Other Notes:				

Fishing Log

Location:_________________________ Date:______________
Location Details: ___________________________________
____
Companions:_______________________________________
Water Temp:_________ Air Temp:________
Hours Fished:________ Wind Direction:________
WInd Speed:________ Humidity:________

Weather ☼ ⚡ ___________________________________
Moon Phase:_______________________________________
Tide Phase:____
Notes:____

Species:	Bait:	Length:	Weight:	Time:
Other Notes:				
Other Notes:				
Other Notes:				
Other Notes:				

Fishing Log

Location:_________________________ Date:______________
Location Details: _______________________________

____
Companions:_____________________________________
Water Temp:__________ Air Temp:________
Hours Fished:________ Wind Direction:________
WInd Speed:________ Humidity:________

Weather ☀ ⚡ _________________________________
Moon Phase:_____________________________________
Tide Phase:_____________________________________
Notes:____

Species:	Bait:	Length:	Weight:	Time:

Other Notes:

Other Notes:

Other Notes:

Other Notes:

Fishing Log

Location:_________________________ Date:____________
Location Details: _________________________________
____
Companions:______________________________________
Water Temp:__________ Air Temp:________
Hours Fished:________ Wind Direction:________
WInd Speed:________ Humidity:________

Weather ☼ ⚡ _______________________________________
Moon Phase:______________________________________
Tide Phase:_______________________________________
Notes:____

Species:	Bait:	Length:	Weight:	Time:

Other Notes:

Other Notes:

Other Notes:

Other Notes:

Fishing Log

Location:_________________________ Date:_______________

Location Details: _________________________________

____

Companions:____

Water Temp:__________ Air Temp:_________

Hours Fished:________ Wind Direction:_________

WInd Speed:________ Humidity:________

Weather ☀⚡ _________________________________

Moon Phase:____

Tide Phase:____

Notes:____

Species:	Bait:	Length:	Weight:	Time:

Other Notes:

Other Notes:

Other Notes:

Other Notes:

Fishing Log

Location:_______________________ Date:____________

Location Details: _______________________________

____

Companions:______________________________________

Water Temp:__________ Air Temp:________

Hours Fished:________ Wind Direction:________

WInd Speed:________ Humidity:________

Weather ____

Moon Phase:______________________________________

Tide Phase:______________________________________

Notes:____

Species:	Bait:	Length:	Weight:	Time:
Other Notes:				
Other Notes:				
Other Notes:				
Other Notes:				

Fishing Log

Location:_________________________ Date:_______________

Location Details: _________________________________

____

Companions:____

Water Temp:___________ Air Temp:_________

Hours Fished:_________ Wind Direction:_________

WInd Speed:_________ Humidity:_________

Weather ☼ ⚡ _______________________________________

Moon Phase:____

Tide Phase:____

Notes:____

Species:	Bait:	Length:	Weight:	Time:

Other Notes:

Other Notes:

Other Notes:

Other Notes:

Fishing Log

Location:_______________________ Date:______________
Location Details: _________________________________

____
Companions:______________________________________
Water Temp:__________ Air Temp:________
Hours Fished:________ Wind Direction:________
WInd Speed:________ Humidity:________

Weather ☼ ⚡ _____________________________________
Moon Phase:______________________________________
Tide Phase:_______________________________________
Notes:____

Species:	Bait:	Length:	Weight:	Time:
Other Notes:				
Other Notes:				
Other Notes:				
Other Notes:				

Fishing Log

Location:___________________________ Date:________________
Location Details: ____

____
Companions:____
Water Temp:___________ Air Temp:_________
Hours Fished:_________ Wind Direction:_________
WInd Speed:_________ Humidity:_________

Weather ☼ ⚡ ____
Moon Phase:____
Tide Phase:____
Notes:____

Species:	Bait:	Length:	Weight:	Time:
Other Notes:				
Other Notes:				
Other Notes:				
Other Notes:				

Fishing Log

Location:_________________________ Date:_____________
Location Details: _______________________________

____

Companions:_______________________________________
Water Temp:___________ Air Temp:_________
Hours Fished:_________ Wind Direction:_________
WInd Speed:_________ Humidity:_________

Weather ☼ ⚡ _______________________________
Moon Phase:_______________________________
Tide Phase:_______________________________
Notes:_______________________________

Species:	Bait:	Length:	Weight:	Time:

Other Notes:

Other Notes:

Other Notes:

Other Notes:

Fishing Log

Location:_________________________ Date:_______________
Location Details: _______________________________________
____
Companions:____
Water Temp:__________ Air Temp:________
Hours Fished:________ Wind Direction:________
WInd Speed:________ Humidity:________

Weather ☀⚡ ____
Moon Phase:____
Tide Phase:____
Notes:____

Species:	Bait:	Length:	Weight:	Time:

Other Notes:

Other Notes:

Other Notes:

Other Notes:

Fishing Log

Location:_______________________ Date:_______________

Location Details: _________________________________

____

Companions:______________________________________

Water Temp:___________ Air Temp:_________

Hours Fished:_________ Wind Direction:_________

WInd Speed:_________ Humidity:_________

Weather ☼ ⚡ _______________________________________

Moon Phase:______________________________________

Tide Phase:_______________________________________

Notes:____

Species:	Bait:	Length:	Weight:	Time:

Other Notes:

Other Notes:

Other Notes:

Other Notes:

Fishing Log

Location:________________________ Date:____________
Location Details: _________________________________
____
Companions:_______________________________________
Water Temp:__________ Air Temp:________
Hours Fished:________ Wind Direction:________
Wlnd Speed:________ Humidity:________

Weather ☼⚡ ___________________________________
Moon Phase:_______________________________________
Tide Phase:_______________________________________
Notes:____

Species:	Bait:	Length:	Weight:	Time:

Other Notes:

Other Notes:

Other Notes:

Other Notes:

Fishing Log

Location:_________________________ Date:______________
Location Details: ________________________________

____
Companions:______________________________________
Water Temp:__________ Air Temp:_______
Hours Fished:________ Wind Direction:_______
WInd Speed:_______ Humidity:_______

Weather ☼ ⚡ _______________________________________
Moon Phase:______________________________________
Tide Phase:_______________________________________
Notes:____

Species:	Bait:	Length:	Weight:	Time:
Other Notes:				
Other Notes:				
Other Notes:				
Other Notes:				

Fishing Log

Location:_____________________ Date:______________

Location Details: ________________________________

____

Companions:_____________________________________

Water Temp:__________ Air Temp:________

Hours Fished:________ Wind Direction:________

WInd Speed:________ Humidity:________

Weather ☀⚡ _________________________________

Moon Phase:_____________________________________

Tide Phase:_____________________________________

Notes:____

Species:	Bait:	Length:	Weight:	Time:

Other Notes:

Other Notes:

Other Notes:

Other Notes:

Fishing Log

Location:_____________________________ Date:_______________
Location Details: ____
____
Companions:____
Water Temp:___________ Air Temp:_________
Hours Fished:_________ Wind Direction:_________
WInd Speed:_________ Humidity:_________

Weather ☀ ⚡ ____
Moon Phase:____
Tide Phase:____
Notes:____

Species:	Bait:	Length:	Weight:	Time:

Other Notes:

Other Notes:

Other Notes:

Other Notes:

Fishing Log

Location:_____________________ Date:_______________

Location Details: _________________________________

____

Companions:______________________________________

Water Temp:__________ Air Temp:________

Hours Fished:________ Wind Direction:________

WInd Speed:________ Humidity:________

Weather ☀⚡ _______________________________________

Moon Phase:______________________________________

Tide Phase:_______________________________________

Notes:____

Species:	Bait:	Length:	Weight:	Time:
Other Notes:				
Other Notes:				
Other Notes:				
Other Notes:				

Fishing Log

Location:_________________________ Date:______________

Location Details: _________________________________

____

Companions:_______________________________________

Water Temp:__________ Air Temp:________

Hours Fished:________ Wind Direction:________

WInd Speed:________ Humidity:________

Weather ☀⚡ _________________________________

Moon Phase:____

Tide Phase:____

Notes:____

Species:	Bait:	Length:	Weight:	Time:

Other Notes:

Other Notes:

Other Notes:

Other Notes:

Fishing Log

Location:________________________ Date:______________

Location Details: _________________________________

____

Companions:______________________________________

Water Temp:__________ Air Temp:________

Hours Fished:________ Wind Direction:________

WInd Speed:________ Humidity:________

Weather ☀⚡ ___________________________________

Moon Phase:______________________________________

Tide Phase:_______________________________________

Notes:____

Species:	Bait:	Length:	Weight:	Time:

Other Notes:

Other Notes:

Other Notes:

Other Notes:

Fishing Log

Location:______________________ Date:______________

Location Details: ________________________________

____

Companions:_____________________________________

Water Temp:__________ Air Temp:________

Hours Fished:________ Wind Direction:________

WInd Speed:________ Humidity:_______

Weather ☼ ⚡ __________________________________

Moon Phase:_____________________________________

Tide Phase:______________________________________

Notes:____

Species:	Bait:	Length:	Weight:	Time:

Other Notes:

Other Notes:

Other Notes:

Other Notes:

Fishing Log

Location:_________________________ Date:______________
Location Details: ________________________________

____
Companions:_______________________________________
Water Temp:__________ Air Temp:________
Hours Fished:________ Wind Direction:________
WInd Speed:________ Humidity:________

Weather ☼ ⚡ _______________________________________
Moon Phase:______________________________________
Tide Phase:_______________________________________
Notes:____

Species:	Bait:	Length:	Weight:	Time:

Other Notes:

Other Notes:

Other Notes:

Other Notes:

Fishing Log

Location:_________________________ Date:______________
Location Details: ___________________________________
____
Companions:____
Water Temp:__________ Air Temp:________
Hours Fished:________ Wind Direction:________
WInd Speed:________ Humidity:________

Weather ☼ ⚡ ____
Moon Phase:____
Tide Phase:____
Notes:____

Species:	Bait:	Length:	Weight:	Time:

Other Notes:

Other Notes:

Other Notes:

Other Notes:

Fishing Log

Location:_______________________ Date:_______________

Location Details: ___________________________________

____

Companions:____

Water Temp:___________ Air Temp:_________

Hours Fished:_________ Wind Direction:_________

WInd Speed:_________ Humidity:_________

Weather ☼ ⚡ ____

Moon Phase:____

Tide Phase:____

Notes:____

Species:	Bait:	Length:	Weight:	Time:

Other Notes:

Other Notes:

Other Notes:

Other Notes:

Fishing Log

Location:_________________________ Date:______________

Location Details: ______________________________________

____

Companions:____

Water Temp:__________ Air Temp:________

Hours Fished:________ Wind Direction:________

WInd Speed:________ Humidity:________

Weather ☀ ⚡ ____

Moon Phase:____

Tide Phase:____

Notes:____

Species:	Bait:	Length:	Weight:	Time:
Other Notes:				
Other Notes:				
Other Notes:				
Other Notes:				

Fishing Log

Location:_____________________ Date:_____________

Location Details: _________________________________

____

Companions:______________________________________

Water Temp:_________ Air Temp:________

Hours Fished:________ Wind Direction:________

WInd Speed:________ Humidity:________

Weather ☼ ⚡ _______________________________

Moon Phase:______________________________________

Tide Phase:_______________________________________

Notes:____

Species:	Bait:	Length:	Weight:	Time:
Other Notes:				
Other Notes:				
Other Notes:				
Other Notes:				

Fishing Log

Location:_______________________ Date:______________

Location Details: ____________________________________

____

Companions:____

Water Temp:__________ Air Temp:_________

Hours Fished:________ Wind Direction:________

WInd Speed:________ Humidity:________

Weather ☼ ⚡ ____

Moon Phase:____

Tide Phase:____

Notes:____

Species:	Bait:	Length:	Weight:	Time:
Other Notes:				
Other Notes:				
Other Notes:				
Other Notes:				

Fishing Log

Location:______________________ Date:______________

Location Details: ________________________________

____

Companions:____

Water Temp:__________ Air Temp:________

Hours Fished:__________ Wind Direction:________

WInd Speed:________ Humidity:________

Weather ☀⚡ _______________________________

Moon Phase:____

Tide Phase:____

Notes:____

Species:	Bait:	Length:	Weight:	Time:
Other Notes:				
Other Notes:				
Other Notes:				
Other Notes:				

Fishing Log

Location:___________________________ Date:_______________

Location Details: ____________________________________

____

Companions:____

Water Temp:__________ Air Temp:________

Hours Fished:________ Wind Direction:________

WInd Speed:________ Humidity:________

Weather ☀ ⚡ ____

Moon Phase:____

Tide Phase:____

Notes:____

Species:	Bait:	Length:	Weight:	Time:
Other Notes:				
Other Notes:				
Other Notes:				
Other Notes:				

Fishing Log

Location:_____________________ Date:_____________

Location Details: _________________________________

____

Companions:______________________________________

Water Temp:__________ Air Temp:________

Hours Fished:________ Wind Direction:________

WInd Speed:________ Humidity:________

Weather ☀ ⚡ ________________________________

Moon Phase:______________________________________

Tide Phase:_______________________________________

Notes:____

Species:	Bait:	Length:	Weight:	Time:
Other Notes:				
Other Notes:				
Other Notes:				
Other Notes:				

Fishing Log

Location:_______________________ Date:______________
Location Details: ___________________________________
____
Companions:____
Water Temp:__________ Air Temp:________
Hours Fished:________ Wind Direction:_______
WInd Speed:________ Humidity:________

Weather ☼⚡_______________________________________
Moon Phase:____
Tide Phase:____
Notes:____

Species:	Bait:	Length:	Weight:	Time:

Other Notes:

Other Notes:

Other Notes:

Other Notes:

Fishing Log

Location:________________________ Date:______________

Location Details: _________________________________

____

Companions:______________________________________

Water Temp:__________ Air Temp:________

Hours Fished:________ Wind Direction:________

WInd Speed:________ Humidity:________

Weather ☼ ⚡ ___________________________________

Moon Phase:______________________________________

Tide Phase:_______________________________________

Notes:____

Species:	Bait:	Length:	Weight:	Time:

Other Notes:

Other Notes:

Other Notes:

Other Notes:

Fishing Log

Location:_____________________ Date:______________

Location Details: _________________________________

____

Companions:______________________________________

Water Temp:__________ Air Temp:_________

Hours Fished:________ Wind Direction:________

WInd Speed:________ Humidity:________

Weather ☼ ⚡ _____________________________________

Moon Phase:______________________________________

Tide Phase:_______________________________________

Notes:____

Species:	Bait:	Length:	Weight:	Time:
Other Notes:				
Other Notes:				
Other Notes:				
Other Notes:				

Fishing Log

Location:________________________ Date:______________
Location Details: _____________________________________

____
Companions:____
Water Temp:__________ Air Temp:________
Hours Fished:________ Wind Direction:________
WInd Speed:________ Humidity:________

Weather ☼ ⚡ ____
Moon Phase:____
Tide Phase:____
Notes:____

Species:	Bait:	Length:	Weight:	Time:

Other Notes:

Other Notes:

Other Notes:

Other Notes:

Fishing Log

Location:_________________________ Date:______________
Location Details: _________________________________
____
Companions:_______________________________________
Water Temp:__________ Air Temp:________
Hours Fished:________ Wind Direction:________
WInd Speed:________ Humidity:________

Weather ☼ ⚡ ____________________________________
Moon Phase:_______________________________________
Tide Phase:____
Notes:____

Species:	Bait:	Length:	Weight:	Time:
Other Notes:				
Other Notes:				
Other Notes:				
Other Notes:				

Fishing Log

Location:_________________________ Date:_______________

Location Details: _______________________________________

____

Companions:____

Water Temp:___________ Air Temp:_________

Hours Fished:_________ Wind Direction:_________

WInd Speed:_________ Humidity:_________

Weather ☼ ⚡ ____

Moon Phase:____

Tide Phase:____

Notes:____

Species:	Bait:	Length:	Weight:	Time:

Other Notes:

Other Notes:

Other Notes:

Other Notes:

Fishing Log

Location:_____________________________ Date:_______________

Location Details: ___________________________________

____

Companions:____

Water Temp:__________ Air Temp:________

Hours Fished:________ Wind Direction:________

WInd Speed:________ Humidity:________

Weather ☀⚡_______________________________________

Moon Phase:____

Tide Phase:____

Notes:____

Species:	Bait:	Length:	Weight:	Time:

Other Notes:

Other Notes:

Other Notes:

Other Notes:

Fishing Log

Location:_________________________ Date:______________
Location Details: ___________________________________
____
Companions:____
Water Temp:___________ Air Temp:__________
Hours Fished:__________ Wind Direction:________
WInd Speed:__________ Humidity:________

Weather ☼ ⚡ _______________________________________
Moon Phase:____
Tide Phase:____
Notes:____

Species:	Bait:	Length:	Weight:	Time:

Other Notes:

Other Notes:

Other Notes:

Other Notes:

Fishing Log

Location:_________________________ Date:______________
Location Details: _________________________________

____
Companions:___________________________________
Water Temp:__________ Air Temp:________
Hours Fished:________ Wind Direction:________
WInd Speed:________ Humidity:________

Weather ☼ ⚡ _____________________________________
Moon Phase:___________________________________
Tide Phase:____________________________________
Notes:____

Species:	Bait:	Length:	Weight:	Time:

Other Notes:

Other Notes:

Other Notes:

Other Notes:

Fishing Log

Location:_________________________ **Date:**_______________

Location Details: ____

____

Companions:____

Water Temp:_________ **Air Temp:**_______

Hours Fished:________ **Wind Direction:**_______

WInd Speed:_______ **Humidity:**_______

Weather ____

Moon Phase:____

Tide Phase:____

Notes:____

Species:	Bait:	Length:	Weight:	Time:

Other Notes:

Other Notes:

Other Notes:

Other Notes:

Fishing Log

Location:_____________________ Date:_____________

Location Details: ____________________________________

____

Companions:____

Water Temp:__________ Air Temp:________

Hours Fished:________ Wind Direction:________

WInd Speed:________ Humidity:________

Weather ☀ ⚡ ____________________________________

Moon Phase:____

Tide Phase:____

Notes:____

Species:	Bait:	Length:	Weight:	Time:

Other Notes:

Other Notes:

Other Notes:

Other Notes:

Fishing Log

Location:_______________________ Date:______________
Location Details: ___________________________________
____
Companions:____
Water Temp:_________ Air Temp:________
Hours Fished:________ Wind Direction:________
WInd Speed:________ Humidity:________

Weather ☼ ⚡ _______________________________________
Moon Phase:____
Tide Phase:____
Notes:____

Species:	Bait:	Length:	Weight:	Time:

Other Notes:

Other Notes:

Other Notes:

Other Notes:

Fishing Log

Location:________________________ Date:______________

Location Details: ________________________________

____

Companions:______________________________________

Water Temp:__________ Air Temp:________

Hours Fished:________ Wind Direction:________

WInd Speed:________ Humidity:________

Weather ☼ ⚡ ________________________________

Moon Phase:______________________________________

Tide Phase:______________________________________

Notes:____

Species:	Bait:	Length:	Weight:	Time:

Other Notes:

Other Notes:

Other Notes:

Other Notes:

Fishing Log

Location:________________________ Date:______________
Location Details: _________________________________

____
Companions:__________________________________
Water Temp:__________ Air Temp:________
Hours Fished:________ Wind Direction:________
WInd Speed:________ Humidity:________

Weather ☀ ⚡ _____________________________________
Moon Phase:_________________________________
Tide Phase:_________________________________
Notes:______________________________________

Species:	Bait:	Length:	Weight:	Time:

Other Notes:

Other Notes:

Other Notes:

Other Notes:

Fishing Log

Location:_______________________ Date:______________

Location Details: ___________________________________

____

Companions:____

Water Temp:__________ Air Temp:_________

Hours Fished:_________ Wind Direction:________

WInd Speed:_________ Humidity:________

Weather ☼ ⚡ ___________________________________

Moon Phase:____

Tide Phase:____

Notes:____

Species:	Bait:	Length:	Weight:	Time:

Other Notes:

Other Notes:

Other Notes:

Other Notes:

Fishing Log

Location:_______________________ Date:_____________
Location Details: ______________________________

____
Companions:_________________________________
Water Temp:_________ Air Temp:_______
Hours Fished:_______ Wind Direction:_______
WInd Speed:_______ Humidity:_______

Weather ☼ ⚡ ____________________________
Moon Phase:_________________________________
Tide Phase:_________________________________
Notes:_____________________________________

Species:	Bait:	Length:	Weight:	Time:
Other Notes:				
Other Notes:				
Other Notes:				
Other Notes:				

Fishing Log

Location:_________________________ Date:_______________

Location Details: ___________________________________

____

Companions:____

Water Temp:__________ Air Temp:_________

Hours Fished:________ Wind Direction:________

WInd Speed:________ Humidity:________

Weather ☼ ⚡ _______________________________________

Moon Phase:____

Tide Phase:____

Notes:____

Species:	Bait:	Length:	Weight:	Time:
Other Notes:				
Other Notes:				
Other Notes:				
Other Notes:				

Fishing Log

Location:_______________________ Date:_______________

Location Details: _________________________________

____

Companions:______________________________________

Water Temp:__________ Air Temp:________

Hours Fished:________ Wind Direction:________

WInd Speed:________ Humidity:________

Weather ☀⚡ _______________________________________

Moon Phase:______________________________________

Tide Phase:_______________________________________

Notes:____

Species:	Bait:	Length:	Weight:	Time:

Other Notes:

Other Notes:

Other Notes:

Other Notes:

Fishing Log

Location:_________________________ Date:_____________
Location Details: ________________________________

____
Companions:______________________________________
Water Temp:___________ Air Temp:_________
Hours Fished:_________ Wind Direction:_________
WInd Speed:_________ Humidity:_________

Weather ☀ ⚡ ________________________________
Moon Phase:______________________________________
Tide Phase:______________________________________
Notes:____

Species:	Bait:	Length:	Weight:	Time:
Other Notes:				
Other Notes:				
Other Notes:				
Other Notes:				

Fishing Log

Location:_________________________ Date:_____________
Location Details: ______________________________________

____
Companions:____
Water Temp:__________ Air Temp:________
Hours Fished:________ Wind Direction:________
WInd Speed:________ Humidity:_______

Weather ☀⚡ ____
Moon Phase:____
Tide Phase:____
Notes:____

Species:	Bait:	Length:	Weight:	Time:

Other Notes:

Other Notes:

Other Notes:

Other Notes:

Fishing Log

Location:_____________________ Date:______________
Location Details: ________________________________

____
Companions:_____________________________________
Water Temp:__________ Air Temp:________
Hours Fished:________ Wind Direction:________
WInd Speed:________ Humidity:________

Weather ☀ ⚡ _________________________________
Moon Phase:_____________________________________
Tide Phase:______________________________________
Notes:____

Species:	Bait:	Length:	Weight:	Time:

Other Notes:

Other Notes:

Other Notes:

Other Notes:

Fishing Log

Location:________________________ Date:____________

Location Details: ______________________________

____

Companions:_____________________________________

Water Temp:__________ Air Temp:________

Hours Fished:________ Wind Direction:________

WInd Speed:________ Humidity:________

Weather ☀⚡ ____________________________________

Moon Phase:_____________________________________

Tide Phase:_____________________________________

Notes:____

Species:	Bait:	Length:	Weight:	Time:

Other Notes:

Other Notes:

Other Notes:

Other Notes:

Fishing Log

Location:_________________________ Date:_____________
Location Details: _________________________________
____
Companions:_____________________________________
Water Temp:__________ Air Temp:________
Hours Fished:________ Wind Direction:________
WInd Speed:________ Humidity:________

Weather ☼ ⚡_________________________________
Moon Phase:_____________________________________
Tide Phase:_____________________________________
Notes:____

Species:	Bait:	Length:	Weight:	Time:

Other Notes:

Other Notes:

Other Notes:

Other Notes:

Fishing Log

Location:_________________________ Date:_______________
Location Details: ____

____

Companions:____
Water Temp:__________ Air Temp:________
Hours Fished:__________ Wind Direction:________
WInd Speed:________ Humidity:________

Weather ☀ ⚡ ____
Moon Phase:____
Tide Phase:____
Notes:____

Species:	Bait:	Length:	Weight:	Time:
Other Notes:				
Other Notes:				
Other Notes:				
Other Notes:				

Fishing Log

Location:_______________________ Date:______________

Location Details: _________________________________

____

Companions:_____________________________________

Water Temp:___________ Air Temp:________

Hours Fished:________ Wind Direction:________

WInd Speed:________ Humidity:________

Weather ☀⚡ _________________________________

Moon Phase:______________________________________

Tide Phase:_______________________________________

Notes:____

Species:	Bait:	Length:	Weight:	Time:

Other Notes:

Other Notes:

Other Notes:

Other Notes:

Fishing Log

Location:_________________________ Date:_____________
Location Details: _________________________________

____
Companions:_______________________________________
Water Temp:_________ Air Temp:________
Hours Fished:________ Wind Direction:________
WInd Speed:________ Humidity:________

Weather ☼ ⚡ _______________________________________
Moon Phase:______________________________________
Tide Phase:______________________________________
Notes:____

Species:	Bait:	Length:	Weight:	Time:
Other Notes:				
Other Notes:				
Other Notes:				
Other Notes:				

Fishing Log

Location:_____________________ Date:_____________

Location Details: _________________________________

____

Companions:______________________________________

Water Temp:__________ Air Temp:________

Hours Fished:________ Wind Direction:________

WInd Speed:________ Humidity:________

Weather ☀ ⚡ ___________________________________

Moon Phase:______________________________________

Tide Phase:_______________________________________

Notes:____

Species:	Bait:	Length:	Weight:	Time:

Other Notes:

Other Notes:

Other Notes:

Other Notes:

Fishing Log

Location:_________________________ Date:______________

Location Details: ________________________________

____

Companions:______________________________________

Water Temp:__________ Air Temp:________

Hours Fished:_________ Wind Direction:________

WInd Speed:________ Humidity:________

Weather ☀⚡ ___________________________________

Moon Phase:______________________________________

Tide Phase:______________________________________

Notes:____

Species:	Bait:	Length:	Weight:	Time:

Other Notes:

Other Notes:

Other Notes:

Other Notes:

Fishing Log

Location:________________________ Date:____________
Location Details: ________________________________
____
Companions:_______________________________________
Water Temp:__________ Air Temp:________
Hours Fished:________ Wind Direction:________
WInd Speed:________ Humidity:________

Weather ☀⚡____
Moon Phase:______________________________________
Tide Phase:______________________________________
Notes:____

Species:	Bait:	Length:	Weight:	Time:

Other Notes:

Other Notes:

Other Notes:

Other Notes:

Fishing Log

Location:_________________________ Date:_______________

Location Details: _____________________________________

____

Companions:____

Water Temp:__________ Air Temp:________

Hours Fished:________ Wind Direction:________

WInd Speed:________ Humidity:________

Weather ☀️⚡ ____________________________________

Moon Phase:____

Tide Phase:____

Notes:____

Species:	Bait:	Length:	Weight:	Time:

Other Notes:

Other Notes:

Other Notes:

Other Notes:

Fishing Log

Location:_______________________ Date:______________
Location Details: _________________________________
____
Companions:______________________________________
Water Temp:__________ Air Temp:________
Hours Fished:________ Wind Direction:________
WInd Speed:________ Humidity:________

Weather ☀ ⚡ ____________________________________
Moon Phase:______________________________________
Tide Phase:_______________________________________
Notes:____

Species:	Bait:	Length:	Weight:	Time:
Other Notes:				
Other Notes:				
Other Notes:				
Other Notes:				

Fishing Log

Location:____________________________ Date:______________
Location Details: ___________________________________

____
Companions:____
Water Temp:__________ Air Temp:________
Hours Fished:________ Wind Direction:________
WInd Speed:________ Humidity:________

Weather ☼ ⚡ _____________________________________
Moon Phase:____
Tide Phase:____
Notes:____

Species:	Bait:	Length:	Weight:	Time:
Other Notes:				
Other Notes:				
Other Notes:				
Other Notes:				

Fishing Log

Location:_______________________ Date:______________

Location Details: ___________________________________

____

Companions:____

Water Temp:__________ Air Temp:________

Hours Fished:________ Wind Direction:________

WInd Speed:________ Humidity:________

Weather ☼ ⚡ ____

Moon Phase:____

Tide Phase:____

Notes:____

Species:	Bait:	Length:	Weight:	Time:
Other Notes:				
Other Notes:				
Other Notes:				
Other Notes:				

Fishing Log

Location:________________________ Date:____________
Location Details: _________________________________

____
Companions:_____________________________________
Water Temp:__________ Air Temp:________
Hours Fished:________ Wind Direction:________
WInd Speed:________ Humidity:________

Weather ☀⚡ _______________________________
Moon Phase:_____________________________________
Tide Phase:_____________________________________
Notes:____

Species:	Bait:	Length:	Weight:	Time:
Other Notes:				
Other Notes:				
Other Notes:				
Other Notes:				

Fishing Log

Location:_________________________ Date:_______________

Location Details: ____

____

Companions:____

Water Temp:___________ Air Temp:_________

Hours Fished:_________ Wind Direction:_________

WInd Speed:_________ Humidity:_________

Weather ☼ ⚡ ____

Moon Phase:____

Tide Phase:____

Notes:____

Species:	Bait:	Length:	Weight:	Time:
Other Notes:				
Other Notes:				
Other Notes:				
Other Notes:				

Fishing Log

Location:_____________________ Date:_____________

Location Details: ___________________________________

____

Companions:____

Water Temp:_________ Air Temp:________

Hours Fished:_______ Wind Direction:________

WInd Speed:_______ Humidity:_______

Weather ☼ ⚡ ___________________________________

Moon Phase:____

Tide Phase:____

Notes:____

Species:	Bait:	Length:	Weight:	Time:

Other Notes:

Other Notes:

Other Notes:

Other Notes:

Fishing Log

Location:_________________________ Date:_____________
Location Details: _________________________________

____
Companions:_______________________________________
Water Temp:__________ Air Temp:_________
Hours Fished:_________ Wind Direction:_________
WInd Speed:_________ Humidity:_________

Weather ☼ ⚡ _____________________________________
Moon Phase:_______________________________________
Tide Phase:_______________________________________
Notes:____

Species:	Bait:	Length:	Weight:	Time:

Other Notes:

Other Notes:

Other Notes:

Other Notes:

Fishing Log

Location:______________________________ Date:_______________

Location Details: ____

____

Companions:____

Water Temp:___________ Air Temp:___________

Hours Fished:_________ Wind Direction:_________

WInd Speed:_________ Humidity:_________

Weather ☀ ⚡ ____

Moon Phase:____

Tide Phase:____

Notes:____

Species:	Bait:	Length:	Weight:	Time:

Other Notes:

Other Notes:

Other Notes:

Other Notes:

Fishing Log

Location:____________________ Date:______________
Location Details: ________________________________
____
Companions:_____________________________________
Water Temp:__________ Air Temp:_________
Hours Fished:_________ Wind Direction:_________
WInd Speed:_________ Humidity:_________

Weather ☼ ⚡ ___________________________________
Moon Phase:_____________________________________
Tide Phase:______________________________________
Notes:____

Species:	Bait:	Length:	Weight:	Time:
Other Notes:				
Other Notes:				
Other Notes:				
Other Notes:				

Fishing Log

Location:____________________ Date:____________
Location Details: _______________________________
____
Companions:_____________________________________
Water Temp:__________ Air Temp:________
Hours Fished:________ Wind Direction:_______
WInd Speed:_______ Humidity:_______

Weather ☼ ⚡ _________________________________
Moon Phase:_____________________________________
Tide Phase:_____________________________________
Notes:____

Species:	Bait:	Length:	Weight:	Time:

Other Notes:

Other Notes:

Other Notes:

Other Notes:

Fishing Log

Location:_________________________ Date:_______________
Location Details: ___________________________________
____
Companions:____
Water Temp:__________ Air Temp:_________
Hours Fished:_________ Wind Direction:_________
WInd Speed:_________ Humidity:_________

Weather ☀ ⚡ ___________________________________
Moon Phase:____
Tide Phase:____
Notes:____

Species:	Bait:	Length:	Weight:	Time:
Other Notes:				
Other Notes:				
Other Notes:				
Other Notes:				

Fishing Log

Location:________________________ Date:______________

Location Details: _________________________________

____

Companions:_____________________________________

Water Temp:__________ Air Temp:________

Hours Fished:________ Wind Direction:________

WInd Speed:________ Humidity:________

Weather ____

Moon Phase:______________________________________

Tide Phase:_______________________________________

Notes:____

Species:	Bait:	Length:	Weight:	Time:

Other Notes:

Other Notes:

Other Notes:

Other Notes:

Fishing Log

Location:_____________________ Date:______________

Location Details: _________________________________

____

Companions:______________________________________

Water Temp:__________ Air Temp:________

Hours Fished:________ Wind Direction:________

WInd Speed:________ Humidity:________

Weather ☼ ⚡ ______________________________________

Moon Phase:______________________________________

Tide Phase:_______________________________________

Notes:____

Species:	Bait:	Length:	Weight:	Time:
Other Notes:				
Other Notes:				
Other Notes:				
Other Notes:				

Fishing Log

Location:_________________________ Date:______________
Location Details: _______________________________________

____

Companions:____
Water Temp:__________ Air Temp:________
Hours Fished:________ Wind Direction:________
WInd Speed:________ Humidity:________

Weather ☀ ⚡ ____
Moon Phase:____
Tide Phase:____
Notes:____

Species:	Bait:	Length:	Weight:	Time:

Other Notes:

Other Notes:

Other Notes:

Other Notes:

Fishing Log

Location:_______________________ Date:______________
Location Details: _________________________________
____
Companions:_____________________________________
Water Temp:__________ Air Temp:________
Hours Fished:________ Wind Direction:________
WInd Speed:________ Humidity:________

Weather ☼ ⚡ _________________________________
Moon Phase:_____________________________________
Tide Phase:______________________________________
Notes:____

Species:	Bait:	Length:	Weight:	Time:
Other Notes:				
Other Notes:				
Other Notes:				
Other Notes:				

Fishing Log

Location:___________________________ Date:_______________
Location Details: ____

____
Companions:____
Water Temp:__________ Air Temp:________
Hours Fished:________ Wind Direction:________
Wind Speed:________ Humidity:________

Weather ☀ ⚡ ____
Moon Phase:____
Tide Phase:____
Notes:____

Species:	Bait:	Length:	Weight:	Time:

Other Notes:

Other Notes:

Other Notes:

Other Notes:

Fishing Log

Location:______________________________ Date:_______________
Location Details: ____
____
Companions:____
Water Temp:___________ Air Temp:_________
Hours Fished:_________ Wind Direction:_________
WInd Speed:_________ Humidity:_________

Weather ☼ ⚡ _______________________________________
Moon Phase:____
Tide Phase:____
Notes:____

Species:	Bait:	Length:	Weight:	Time:

Other Notes:

Other Notes:

Other Notes:

Other Notes:

Fishing Log

Location:_____________________________ Date:_______________

Location Details: _______________________________________

____

Companions:____

Water Temp:___________ Air Temp:_________

Hours Fished:_________ Wind Direction:_________

WInd Speed:_________ Humidity:_________

Weather ☀ ⚡ ____

Moon Phase:____

Tide Phase:____

Notes:____

Species:	Bait:	Length:	Weight:	Time:
Other Notes:				
Other Notes:				
Other Notes:				
Other Notes:				

Fishing Log

Location:_________________________ Date:______________
Location Details: _________________________________

____
Companions:_____________________________________
Water Temp:_________ Air Temp:________
Hours Fished:_______ Wind Direction:_______
WInd Speed:_______ Humidity:_______

Weather ☼ ⚡ ______________________________________
Moon Phase:____________________________________
Tide Phase:_____________________________________
Notes:____

Species:	Bait:	Length:	Weight:	Time:

Other Notes:

Other Notes:

Other Notes:

Other Notes:

Fishing Log

Location:_____________________________ Date:_______________

Location Details: ____

____

Companions:____

Water Temp:__________ Air Temp:________

Hours Fished:________ Wind Direction:________

WInd Speed:________ Humidity:________

Weather ☀ ⚡ ____

Moon Phase:____

Tide Phase:____

Notes:____

Species:	Bait:	Length:	Weight:	Time:

Other Notes:

Other Notes:

Other Notes:

Other Notes:

Fishing Log

Location:_____________________________ Date:______________
Location Details: ____

____
Companions:____
Water Temp:__________ Air Temp:________
Hours Fished:________ Wind Direction:________
WInd Speed:________ Humidity:________

Weather ☀ ⚡ ____
Moon Phase:____
Tide Phase:____
Notes:____

Species:	Bait:	Length:	Weight:	Time:

Other Notes:

Other Notes:

Other Notes:

Other Notes:

Fishing Log

Location:_____________________ Date:_____________

Location Details: ___________________________________

____

Companions:____

Water Temp:__________ Air Temp:________

Hours Fished:________ Wind Direction:________

WInd Speed:________ Humidity:________

Weather ☀⚡ ____

Moon Phase:____

Tide Phase:____

Notes:____

Species:	Bait:	Length:	Weight:	Time:

Other Notes:

Other Notes:

Other Notes:

Other Notes:

Fishing Log

Location:_____________________ Date:______________

Location Details: _________________________________

____

Companions:______________________________________

Water Temp:_________ Air Temp:________

Hours Fished:________ Wind Direction:_______

WInd Speed:________ Humidity:________

Weather ☀ ⚡ ________________________________

Moon Phase:______________________________________

Tide Phase:_______________________________________

Notes:____

Species:	Bait:	Length:	Weight:	Time:
Other Notes:				
Other Notes:				
Other Notes:				
Other Notes:				

Fishing Log

Location:_______________________ Date:_______________

Location Details: _________________________________

____

Companions:______________________________________

Water Temp:__________ Air Temp:_________

Hours Fished:________ Wind Direction:________

WInd Speed:________ Humidity:________

Weather ☼ ⚡ _____________________________________

Moon Phase:______________________________________

Tide Phase:______________________________________

Notes:____

Species:	Bait:	Length:	Weight:	Time:
Other Notes:				
Other Notes:				
Other Notes:				
Other Notes:				

Fishing Log

Location:____________________ Date:____________
Location Details: _________________________________
____
Companions:____
Water Temp:__________ Air Temp:________
Hours Fished:________ Wind Direction:________
WInd Speed:________ Humidity:________

Weather ☀ ⚡ _______________________________________
Moon Phase:____
Tide Phase:____
Notes:____

Species:	Bait:	Length:	Weight:	Time:

Other Notes:

Other Notes:

Other Notes:

Other Notes:

Fishing Log

Location:_______________________ Date:_____________
Location Details: ____________________________________

____
Companions:____
Water Temp:__________ Air Temp:________
Hours Fished:________ Wind Direction:________
WInd Speed:________ Humidity:________

Weather ☼ ⚡ ____
Moon Phase:____
Tide Phase:____
Notes:____

Species:	Bait:	Length:	Weight:	Time:

Other Notes:

Other Notes:

Other Notes:

Other Notes:

Fishing Log

Location:__________________________ Date:_______________

Location Details: ____

____

Companions:____

Water Temp:__________ Air Temp:________

Hours Fished:________ Wind Direction:________

WInd Speed:________ Humidity:________

Weather ☼ ⚡ ____

Moon Phase:____

Tide Phase:____

Notes:____

Species:	Bait:	Length:	Weight:	Time:

Other Notes:

Other Notes:

Other Notes:

Other Notes:

Fishing Log

Location:____________________ Date:____________

Location Details: ____________________________________

____

Companions:____

Water Temp:__________ Air Temp:________

Hours Fished:________ Wind Direction:________

WInd Speed:________ Humidity:________

Weather ☼ ⚡ ____________________________________

Moon Phase:____

Tide Phase:____

Notes:____

Species:	Bait:	Length:	Weight:	Time:

Other Notes:

Other Notes:

Other Notes:

Other Notes:

Fishing Log

Location:_________________________ Date:______________
Location Details: _________________________________
____
Companions:______________________________________
Water Temp:__________ Air Temp:________
Hours Fished:________ Wind Direction:________
WInd Speed:________ Humidity:________

Weather ☼ ⚡ ____________________________________
Moon Phase:______________________________________
Tide Phase:______________________________________
Notes:____

Species:	Bait:	Length:	Weight:	Time:
Other Notes:				
Other Notes:				
Other Notes:				
Other Notes:				

Fishing Log

Location:_______________________ Date:______________

Location Details: _________________________________

____

Companions:______________________________________

Water Temp:__________ Air Temp:________

Hours Fished:________ Wind Direction:________

WInd Speed:________ Humidity:________

Weather ☼ ⚡ _________________________________

Moon Phase:______________________________________

Tide Phase:______________________________________

Notes:____

Species:	Bait:	Length:	Weight:	Time:

Other Notes:

Other Notes:

Other Notes:

Other Notes:

Fishing Log

Location:_________________________ Date:______________

Location Details: _________________________________

____

Companions:______________________________________

Water Temp:_________ Air Temp:_______

Hours Fished:_______ Wind Direction:_______

WInd Speed:_______ Humidity:_______

Weather ☀ ⚡ _______________________________

Moon Phase:______________________________________

Tide Phase:_______________________________________

Notes:____

Species:	Bait:	Length:	Weight:	Time:

Other Notes:

Other Notes:

Other Notes:

Other Notes:

Fishing Log

Location:________________________ Date:______________

Location Details: ________________________________

____

Companions:_____________________________________

Water Temp:__________ Air Temp:________

Hours Fished:________ Wind Direction:________

WInd Speed:________ Humidity:________

Weather ☀ ⚡ ______________________________________

Moon Phase:_____________________________________

Tide Phase:______________________________________

Notes:____

Species:	Bait:	Length:	Weight:	Time:

Other Notes:

Other Notes:

Other Notes:

Other Notes:

Fishing Log

Location:________________________ Date:____________

Location Details: _________________________________

____

Companions:______________________________________

Water Temp:__________ Air Temp:________

Hours Fished:________ Wind Direction:________

WInd Speed:________ Humidity:________

Weather ☼ ⚡ _____________________________________

Moon Phase:______________________________________

Tide Phase:_______________________________________

Notes:____

Species:	Bait:	Length:	Weight:	Time:
Other Notes:				
Other Notes:				
Other Notes:				
Other Notes:				

Fishing Log

Location:___________________________ Date:______________

Location Details: _______________________________

____

Companions:_______________________________________

Water Temp:___________ Air Temp:_________

Hours Fished:_________ Wind Direction:_________

WInd Speed:_________ Humidity:_________

Weather ☼ ⚡ _____________________________________

Moon Phase:_______________________________________

Tide Phase:____

Notes:____

Species:	Bait:	Length:	Weight:	Time:

Other Notes:

Other Notes:

Other Notes:

Other Notes:

Fishing Log

Location:_____________________________ Date:_______________

Location Details: _______________________________________

____

Companions:____

Water Temp:__________ Air Temp:________

Hours Fished:_________ Wind Direction:________

WInd Speed:________ Humidity:________

Weather ☼ ⚡ ____

Moon Phase:____

Tide Phase:____

Notes:____

Species:	Bait:	Length:	Weight:	Time:
Other Notes:				
Other Notes:				
Other Notes:				
Other Notes:				

Fishing Log

Location:_______________________ Date:_____________

Location Details: _________________________________

____

Companions:_______________________________________

Water Temp:__________ Air Temp:________

Hours Fished:________ Wind Direction:________

WInd Speed:________ Humidity:________

Weather ☼ ⚡ ___________________________________

Moon Phase:_______________________________________

Tide Phase:_______________________________________

Notes:____

Species:	Bait:	Length:	Weight:	Time:
Other Notes:				
Other Notes:				
Other Notes:				
Other Notes:				

Fishing Log

Location:_________________________ Date:______________
Location Details: _______________________________________

____
Companions:____
Water Temp:__________ Air Temp:________
Hours Fished:________ Wind Direction:________
WInd Speed:________ Humidity:________

Weather ☼ ⚡ ____
Moon Phase:____
Tide Phase:____
Notes:____

Species:	Bait:	Length:	Weight:	Time:

Other Notes:

Other Notes:

Other Notes:

Other Notes:

Fishing Log

Location:_________________________ Date:______________
Location Details: ______________________________________
____
Companions:____
Water Temp:__________ Air Temp:________
Hours Fished:________ Wind Direction:________
WInd Speed:________ Humidity:________

Weather ☀⚡ ______________________________________
Moon Phase:____
Tide Phase:____
Notes:____

Species:	Bait:	Length:	Weight:	Time:

Other Notes:

Other Notes:

Other Notes:

Other Notes:

Fishing Log

Location:_____________________________ Date:_______________
Location Details: ____

____
Companions:____
Water Temp:___________ Air Temp:_________
Hours Fished:_________ Wind Direction:_________
WInd Speed:_________ Humidity:_________

Weather ☼ ⚡ ____
Moon Phase:____
Tide Phase:____
Notes:____

Species:	Bait:	Length:	Weight:	Time:
Other Notes:				
Other Notes:				
Other Notes:				
Other Notes:				

Fishing Log

Location:________________________ Date:______________

Location Details: ____________________________________

____

Companions:____

Water Temp:__________ Air Temp:________

Hours Fished:________ Wind Direction:________

WInd Speed:________ Humidity:________

Weather ☼ ⚡ _______________________________________

Moon Phase:____

Tide Phase:____

Notes:____

Species:	Bait:	Length:	Weight:	Time:

Other Notes:

Other Notes:

Other Notes:

Other Notes:

Fishing Log

Location:_________________________ Date:______________
Location Details: ____

____
Companions:____
Water Temp:__________ Air Temp:_________
Hours Fished:_________ Wind Direction:_________
WInd Speed:_________ Humidity:_________

Weather ☼ ⚡ _______________________________________
Moon Phase:____
Tide Phase:____
Notes:____

Species:	Bait:	Length:	Weight:	Time:
Other Notes:				
Other Notes:				
Other Notes:				
Other Notes:				

Fishing Log

Location:________________________ Date:______________
Location Details: _________________________________

____

Companions:____
Water Temp:__________ Air Temp:__________
Hours Fished:__________ Wind Direction:__________
WInd Speed:__________ Humidity:__________

Weather ☀ ⚡ ___________________________________
Moon Phase:____
Tide Phase:____
Notes:____

Species:	Bait:	Length:	Weight:	Time:

Other Notes:

Other Notes:

Other Notes:

Other Notes:

Fishing Log

Location:________________________ Date:____________
Location Details: ________________________________

____
Companions:______________________________________
Water Temp:__________ Air Temp:________
Hours Fished:________ Wind Direction:________
WInd Speed:________ Humidity:________

Weather ☼ ⚡ ________________________________
Moon Phase:______________________________________
Tide Phase:______________________________________
Notes:____

Species:	Bait:	Length:	Weight:	Time:

Other Notes:

Other Notes:

Other Notes:

Other Notes:

Fishing Log

Location:_________________________ Date:_____________
Location Details: _________________________________

____
Companions:_______________________________________
Water Temp:__________ Air Temp:________
Hours Fished:________ Wind Direction:________
WInd Speed:________ Humidity:________

Weather ☼ ⚡ _________________________________
Moon Phase:_______________________________________
Tide Phase:____
Notes:____

Species:	Bait:	Length:	Weight:	Time:
Other Notes:				
Other Notes:				
Other Notes:				
Other Notes:				

Fishing Log

Location:_____________________ Date:_____________

Location Details: _________________________________

____

Companions:______________________________________

Water Temp:__________ Air Temp:________

Hours Fished:________ Wind Direction:________

WInd Speed:________ Humidity:________

Weather ☀ ⚡ _______________________________

Moon Phase:______________________________________

Tide Phase:_______________________________________

Notes:____

Species:	Bait:	Length:	Weight:	Time:
Other Notes:				
Other Notes:				
Other Notes:				
Other Notes:				

Fishing Log

Location:_________________________ Date:_______________

Location Details: ___________________________________

____

Companions:____

Water Temp:__________ Air Temp:________

Hours Fished:________ Wind Direction:________

WInd Speed:________ Humidity:________

Weather ☀ ⚡ ____________________________________

Moon Phase:____

Tide Phase:____

Notes:____

Species:	Bait:	Length:	Weight:	Time:

Other Notes:

Other Notes:

Other Notes:

Other Notes:

Fishing Log

Location:_____________________ Date:_____________
Location Details: _________________________________
____
Companions:_____________________________________
Water Temp:__________ Air Temp:________
Hours Fished:________ Wind Direction:________
WInd Speed:________ Humidity:________

Weather ☀⚡ _____________________________________
Moon Phase:______________________________________
Tide Phase:_______________________________________
Notes:____

Species:	Bait:	Length:	Weight:	Time:

Other Notes:

Other Notes:

Other Notes:

Other Notes:

Fishing Log

Location:_________________________ Date:______________
Location Details: ____

____
Companions:____
Water Temp:___________ Air Temp:_________
Hours Fished:_________ Wind Direction:_________
WInd Speed:_________ Humidity:_________

Weather ☼ ⚡ _______________________________________
Moon Phase:____
Tide Phase:____
Notes:____

Species:	Bait:	Length:	Weight:	Time:

Other Notes:

Other Notes:

Other Notes:

Other Notes:

Fishing Log

Location:_________________________ Date:_______________
Location Details: _______________________________________

____
Companions:____
Water Temp:__________ Air Temp:_________
Hours Fished:________ Wind Direction:________
WInd Speed:________ Humidity:________

Weather ☼ ⚡ ______________________________________
Moon Phase:____
Tide Phase:____
Notes:____

Species:	Bait:	Length:	Weight:	Time:

Other Notes:

Other Notes:

Other Notes:

Other Notes:

Fishing Log

Location:_______________________ Date:____________
Location Details: ______________________________

____
Companions:_____________________________________
Water Temp:__________ Air Temp:________
Hours Fished:________ Wind Direction:________
WInd Speed:________ Humidity:________

Weather ☀ ⚡ _______________________________
Moon Phase:____________________________________
Tide Phase:_____________________________________
Notes:____

Species:	Bait:	Length:	Weight:	Time:

Other Notes:

Other Notes:

Other Notes:

Other Notes:

Fishing Log

Location:________________________ Date:____________
Location Details: _________________________________

____
Companions:_____________________________________
Water Temp:__________ Air Temp:________
Hours Fished:________ Wind Direction:________
WInd Speed:________ Humidity:________

Weather ☀⚡ __________________________________
Moon Phase:_____________________________________
Tide Phase:_____________________________________
Notes:____

Species:	Bait:	Length:	Weight:	Time:
Other Notes:				
Other Notes:				
Other Notes:				
Other Notes:				

Fishing Log

Location:______________________ Date:______________
Location Details: _________________________________
____
Companions:_____________________________________
Water Temp:__________ Air Temp:________
Hours Fished:________ Wind Direction:________
WInd Speed:________ Humidity:________

Weather ☼ ⚡ ________________________________
Moon Phase:____________________________________
Tide Phase:_____________________________________
Notes:____

Species:	Bait:	Length:	Weight:	Time:
Other Notes:				
Other Notes:				
Other Notes:				
Other Notes:				

Fishing Log

Location:_________________________ Date:_______________

Location Details: _______________________________________

____

Companions:____

Water Temp:__________ Air Temp:________

Hours Fished:________ Wind Direction:________

WInd Speed:________ Humidity:________

Weather ☼ ⚡ ____

Moon Phase:____

Tide Phase:____

Notes:____

Species:	Bait:	Length:	Weight:	Time:
Other Notes:				
Other Notes:				
Other Notes:				
Other Notes:				

Fishing Log

Location:___________________ Date:______________

Location Details: _____________________________

____

Companions:____________________________________

Water Temp:__________ Air Temp:________

Hours Fished:_______ Wind Direction:_______

WInd Speed:_______ Humidity:________

Weather ☼ ⚡ _________________________________

Moon Phase:____________________________________

Tide Phase:____________________________________

Notes:____

Species:	Bait:	Length:	Weight:	Time:
Other Notes:				
Other Notes:				
Other Notes:				
Other Notes:				

Fishing Log

Location:_______________________ Date:______________

Location Details: ________________________________
____

Companions:______________________________________

Water Temp:__________ Air Temp:________

Hours Fished:________ Wind Direction:________

WInd Speed:________ Humidity:________

Weather ☀ ⚡ _________________________________

Moon Phase:______________________________________

Tide Phase:______________________________________

Notes:____

Species:	Bait:	Length:	Weight:	Time:

Other Notes:

Other Notes:

Other Notes:

Other Notes:

Fishing Log

Location:_________________________ Date:_______________
Location Details: ____

____
Companions:____
Water Temp:__________ Air Temp:________
Hours Fished:________ Wind Direction:________
WInd Speed:________ Humidity:________

Weather ☼ ⚡ ____
Moon Phase:____
Tide Phase:____
Notes:____

Species:	Bait:	Length:	Weight:	Time:

Other Notes:

Other Notes:

Other Notes:

Other Notes:

Fishing Log

Location:_________________________ Date:______________
Location Details: _________________________________

____
Companions:_______________________________________
Water Temp:__________ Air Temp:________
Hours Fished:________ Wind Direction:________
WInd Speed:________ Humidity:________

Weather ☼ ⚡ _____________________________________
Moon Phase:______________________________________
Tide Phase:_______________________________________
Notes:____

Species:	Bait:	Length:	Weight:	Time:
Other Notes:				
Other Notes:				
Other Notes:				
Other Notes:				

Fishing Log

Location:_________________________ Date:______________
Location Details: _________________________________

____
Companions:_______________________________________
Water Temp:_________ Air Temp:_______
Hours Fished:_______ Wind Direction:_______
WInd Speed:_______ Humidity:_______

Weather ☀ ⚡ _____________________________________
Moon Phase:______________________________________
Tide Phase:_______________________________________
Notes:____

Species:	Bait:	Length:	Weight:	Time:
Other Notes:				
Other Notes:				
Other Notes:				
Other Notes:				

Fishing Log

Location:______________________ Date:______________

Location Details: ___________________________________

____

Companions:____

Water Temp:__________ Air Temp:________

Hours Fished:________ Wind Direction:________

WInd Speed:________ Humidity:________

Weather ☀ ⚡ ___________________________________

Moon Phase:____

Tide Phase:____

Notes:____

Species:	Bait:	Length:	Weight:	Time:

Other Notes:

Other Notes:

Other Notes:

Other Notes:

Fishing Log

Location:_________________________ Date:_______________

Location Details: _______________________________________

____

Companions:____

Water Temp:__________ Air Temp:________

Hours Fished:________ Wind Direction:________

WInd Speed:________ Humidity:________

Weather ☼ ⚡ ____

Moon Phase:____

Tide Phase:____

Notes:____

Species:	Bait:	Length:	Weight:	Time:

Other Notes:

Other Notes:

Other Notes:

Other Notes:

Fishing Log

Location:_________________________ Date:______________

Location Details: _________________________________

____

Companions:____

Water Temp:__________ Air Temp:________

Hours Fished:________ Wind Direction:________

WInd Speed:________ Humidity:________

Weather ☼ ⚡ ___________________________________

Moon Phase:____

Tide Phase:____

Notes:____

Species:	Bait:	Length:	Weight:	Time:

Other Notes:

Other Notes:

Other Notes:

Other Notes:

Fishing Log

Location:________________________ Date:______________
Location Details: ___________________________________

____
Companions:____
Water Temp:__________ Air Temp:________
Hours Fished:________ Wind Direction:_______
WInd Speed:________ Humidity:________

Weather ☀ ⚡ ____
Moon Phase:____
Tide Phase:____
Notes:____

Species:	Bait:	Length:	Weight:	Time:

Other Notes:

Other Notes:

Other Notes:

Other Notes:

Fishing Log

Location:_______________________ Date:______________

Location Details: ___________________________________

____

Companions:____

Water Temp:__________ Air Temp:________

Hours Fished:________ Wind Direction:________

WInd Speed:________ Humidity:________

Weather ☀⚡ _________________________________

Moon Phase:____

Tide Phase:____

Notes:____

Species:	Bait:	Length:	Weight:	Time:

Other Notes:

Other Notes:

Other Notes:

Other Notes:

Fishing Log

Location:_____________________ Date:_____________

Location Details: ________________________________

____

Companions:______________________________________

Water Temp:_________ Air Temp:_______

Hours Fished:_______ Wind Direction:_______

WInd Speed:_______ Humidity:_______

Weather ☀ ⚡ ______________________________________

Moon Phase:______________________________________

Tide Phase:_______________________________________

Notes:____

Species:	Bait:	Length:	Weight:	Time:

Other Notes:

Other Notes:

Other Notes:

Other Notes:

Fishing Log

Location:_________________________ Date:________________
Location Details: ______________________________________

____
Companions:____
Water Temp:__________ Air Temp:________
Hours Fished:________ Wind Direction:________
WInd Speed:________ Humidity:________

Weather ☀ ⚡ ____
Moon Phase:____
Tide Phase:____
Notes:____

Species:	Bait:	Length:	Weight:	Time:
Other Notes:				
Other Notes:				
Other Notes:				
Other Notes:				

Fishing Log

Location:____________________ Date:______________
Location Details: ________________________________

____
Companions:_______________________________________
Water Temp:__________ Air Temp:________
Hours Fished:________ Wind Direction:________
WInd Speed:________ Humidity:________

Weather ☼ ⚡ ______________________________________
Moon Phase:_______________________________________
Tide Phase:_______________________________________
Notes:____

Species:	Bait:	Length:	Weight:	Time:

Other Notes:

Other Notes:

Other Notes:

Other Notes:

Fishing Log

Location:_________________________ Date:______________
Location Details: _________________________________

____
Companions:_______________________________________
Water Temp:__________ Air Temp:________
Hours Fished:________ Wind Direction:________
WInd Speed:________ Humidity:________

Weather ☀⚡ _________________________________
Moon Phase:_______________________________________
Tide Phase:_______________________________________
Notes:____

Species:	Bait:	Length:	Weight:	Time:

Other Notes:

Other Notes:

Other Notes:

Other Notes:

Fishing Log

Location:_____________________ Date:_____________

Location Details: _________________________

____

Companions:_________________________________

Water Temp:_________ Air Temp:_______

Hours Fished:_______ Wind Direction:_______

WInd Speed:_______ Humidity:_______

Weather ☼ ⚡ _________________________

Moon Phase:_______________________________

Tide Phase:_______________________________

Notes:_____________________________________

Species:	Bait:	Length:	Weight:	Time:

Other Notes:

Other Notes:

Other Notes:

Other Notes:

Fishing Log

Location:_________________________ Date:_______________
Location Details: ____

____
Companions:____
Water Temp:__________ Air Temp:________
Hours Fished:________ Wind Direction:________
WInd Speed:________ Humidity:________

Weather ☼ ⚡____
Moon Phase:____
Tide Phase:____
Notes:____

Species:	Bait:	Length:	Weight:	Time:
Other Notes:				
Other Notes:				
Other Notes:				
Other Notes:				

Fishing Log

Location:_______________________ Date:______________

Location Details: _____________________________________

____

Companions:____

Water Temp:___________ Air Temp:_________

Hours Fished:_________ Wind Direction:________

WInd Speed:_________ Humidity:________

Weather ☼ ⚡____

Moon Phase:____

Tide Phase:____

Notes:____

Species:	Bait:	Length:	Weight:	Time:
Other Notes:				
Other Notes:				
Other Notes:				
Other Notes:				

Fishing Log

Location:_________________________ Date:______________
Location Details: ___________________________________

____
Companions:____
Water Temp:___________ Air Temp:_________
Hours Fished:_________ Wind Direction:_________
WInd Speed:_________ Humidity:_________

Weather ☀⚡ _______________________________________
Moon Phase:____
Tide Phase:____
Notes:____

Species:	Bait:	Length:	Weight:	Time:
Other Notes:				
Other Notes:				
Other Notes:				
Other Notes:				

Fishing Log

Location:___________________ Date:____________
Location Details: ____________________________
____
Companions:____________________________________
Water Temp:_________ Air Temp:________
Hours Fished:________ Wind Direction:_______
WInd Speed:________ Humidity:________

Weather ☼ ⚡ ______________________________________
Moon Phase:____________________________________
Tide Phase:_____________________________________
Notes:____

Species:	Bait:	Length:	Weight:	Time:

Other Notes:

Other Notes:

Other Notes:

Other Notes:

Fishing Log

Location:_________________________ Date:______________

Location Details: _________________________________

____

Companions:_______________________________________

Water Temp:__________ Air Temp:________

Hours Fished:________ Wind Direction:________

WInd Speed:________ Humidity:________

Weather ☼ ⚡ _________________________________

Moon Phase:_______________________________________

Tide Phase:____

Notes:____

Species:	Bait:	Length:	Weight:	Time:

Other Notes:

Other Notes:

Other Notes:

Other Notes:

Fishing Log

Location:_________________________ Date:______________

Location Details: ________________________________

____

Companions:_____________________________________

Water Temp:__________ Air Temp:_________

Hours Fished:________ Wind Direction:________

Wind Speed:________ Humidity:________

Weather ☼ ⚡ _______________________________

Moon Phase:_____________________________________

Tide Phase:______________________________________

Notes:____

Species:	Bait:	Length:	Weight:	Time:

Other Notes:

Other Notes:

Other Notes:

Other Notes:

Fishing Log

Location:_________________________ Date:_______________
Location Details: ___________________________________

____
Companions:____
Water Temp:__________ Air Temp:________
Hours Fished:________ Wind Direction:________
WInd Speed:________ Humidity:________

Weather ☼ ⚡ _______________________________________
Moon Phase:____
Tide Phase:____
Notes:____

Species:	Bait:	Length:	Weight:	Time:
Other Notes:				
Other Notes:				
Other Notes:				
Other Notes:				

Fishing Log

Location:_________________________ Date:_______________

Location Details: _____________________________________

____

Companions:____

Water Temp:__________ Air Temp:________

Hours Fished:________ Wind Direction:_______

WInd Speed:________ Humidity:________

Weather ____

Moon Phase:____

Tide Phase:____

Notes:____

Species:	Bait:	Length:	Weight:	Time:

Other Notes:

Other Notes:

Other Notes:

Other Notes:

Fishing Log

Location:_________________________ Date:________________

Location Details: ____

____

Companions:____

Water Temp:___________ Air Temp:_________

Hours Fished:_________ Wind Direction:________

WInd Speed:________ Humidity:________

Weather ☀️⚡ _____________________________________

Moon Phase:____

Tide Phase:____

Notes:____

Species:	Bait:	Length:	Weight:	Time:

Other Notes:

Other Notes:

Other Notes:

Other Notes:

Fishing Log

Location:_____________________ Date:_______________

Location Details: _________________________________

____

Companions:_______________________________________

Water Temp:__________ Air Temp:_________

Hours Fished:________ Wind Direction:_______

WInd Speed:________ Humidity:________

Weather ☀ ⚡ _______________________________________

Moon Phase:_______________________________________

Tide Phase:_______________________________________

Notes:____

Species:	Bait:	Length:	Weight:	Time:

Other Notes:

Other Notes:

Other Notes:

Other Notes:

Other Notes:

Fishing Log

Location:_________________________ Date:_______________

Location Details: _______________________________________

____

Companions:____

Water Temp:___________ Air Temp:_________

Hours Fished:_________ Wind Direction:_________

WInd Speed:_________ Humidity:_________

Weather ☼ ⚡ ____

Moon Phase:____

Tide Phase:____

Notes:____

Species:	Bait:	Length:	Weight:	Time:

Other Notes:

Other Notes:

Other Notes:

Other Notes:

9 781651 665367